APR -- 2017			
		PRINTED IN U.S.A.	

IOWA

The Hawkeye State

BY
JOHN HAMILTON

Abdo & Daughters

An imprint of Abdo Publishing | abdopublishing.com

abdopublishing.com

Published by ABDO Publishing, a division of ABDO, PO Box 398166, Minneapolis, Minnesota 55439. Copyright © 2017 by Abdo Consulting Group, Inc. International copyrights reserved in all countries. No part of this book may be reproduced in any form without written permission from the publisher. ABDO & Daughters™ is a trademark and logo of ABDO Publishing.

Printed in the United States of America, North Mankato, Minnesota.
012016
092016

THIS BOOK CONTAINS
RECYCLED MATERIALS

Editor: Sue Hamilton **Contributing Editor:** Bridget O'Brien
Graphic Design: Sue Hamilton
Cover Art Direction: Candice Keimig **Cover Photo Selection:** Neil Klinepier
Cover Photo: iStock
Interior Images: Alamy, AP, Blank Park Zoo, City of Sioux City, Corbis, Des Moines Register, Dr. Macro, Dreamstime, Glow Images, Iowa Natural Heritage Foundation, History in Full Color-Restoration/Colorization, Iowa State Fair, Iowa State University, iStock, John Hamilton, Library of Congress, Mile High Maps, NASA, National Park Service, North Wind, One Mile Up, US Geological Survey, US Naval Historical Center, University of Iowa-Dept of Athletics, Wikimedia.

Statistics: *State and City Populations*, U.S. Census Bureau, July 1, 2014 estimates; *Land and Water Area*, U.S. Census Bureau, 2010 Census, MAF/TIGER database; *State Temperature Extremes*, NOAA National Climatic Data Center; *Climatology and Average Annual Precipitation*, NOAA National Climatic Data Center, 1980-2015 statewide averages; *State Highest and Lowest Points*, NOAA National Geodetic Survey.

Websites: To learn more about the United States, visit booklinks.abdopublishing.com. These links are routinely monitored and updated to provide the most current information available.

Cataloging-in-Publication Data
Names: Hamilton, John, 1959- author.
Title: Iowa / by John Hamilton.
Description: Minneapolis, MN : Abdo Publishing, [2017] | Series: The United
    States of America | Includes index.
Identifiers: LCCN 201597604 | ISBN 9781680783179 (lib. bdg.) |
    ISBN 9781680774214 (ebook)
Subjects: LCSH: Iowa--Juvenile literature.
Classification: DDC 977.7--dc23
LC record available at http://lccn.loc.gov/201597604

CONTENTS

THE
HAWKEYE
STATE

Iowa is a land of surprises. There are many farms and small towns. The state's gently rolling hills are filled with row after row of corn and soybeans. But there's more to the state than barns and tractors. Iowa is a rural state, but students flock to its world-class colleges and universities. In bustling cities like Des Moines, Iowa City, and Ames, there are museums, zoos, parks, concert halls, sports stadiums, and ethnic restaurants.

Iowans pride themselves on their friendliness. Drivers wave as they pass each other on country roads. When someone is in need, neighbors are quick to lend a hand, or offer a steaming casserole for dinner.

Iowa's nickname is "The Hawkeye State." It is named partly after the fictional character Hawkeye in James Fenimore Cooper's novel *The Last of the Mohicans*. It is also named in honor of Black Hawk, a Native American leader of the Sauk tribe.

A statue called "The Pioneers" overlooks Des Moines, Iowa.

An Iowa farm on the bluffs above the Mississippi River in Dubuque County, Iowa.

QUICK FACTS

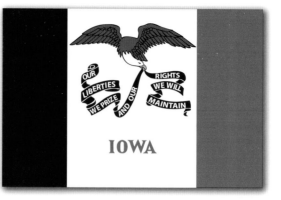

Name: Iowa gets its name from a tribe of Native Americans that early European explorers called the Ioway.

State Capital: Des Moines, population 209,220

Date of Statehood: December 28, 1846 (29th state)

Population: 3,107,126 (30th-most populous state)

Area (Total Land and Water): 56,273 square miles (145,746 sq km), 26th-largest state

Largest City: Des Moines, population 209,220

Nickname: The Hawkeye State

Motto: Our liberties we prize and our rights we will maintain

State Bird: Eastern Goldfinch

State Flower: Wild Rose

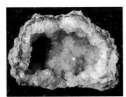

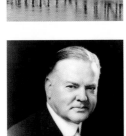

State Rock: Geode

State Tree: Oak

State Song: "Song of Iowa"

Highest Point: Hawkeye Point in Osceola County, 1,670 feet (509 m)

Lowest Point: 480 feet (146 m) on the Mississippi River in Lee County

Average July High Temperature: 84°F (29°C)

Record High Temperature: 118°F (48°C), in Keokuk on July 20, 1934

Average January Low Temperature: 11°F (-12°C)

Record Low Temperature: -47°F (-44°C), on January 12, 1912, in Washta, and on February 3, 1996, in Elkader

Average Annual Precipitation: 34 inches (86 cm)

Number of U.S. Senators: 2

Number of U.S. Representatives: 4

U.S. Presidents Born in Iowa: Herbert Hoover (1874-1964), 31st president

U.S. Postal Service Abbreviation: IA

Herbert Hoover

GEOGRAPHY

Iowa is a state in the Midwest. It is in the north central part of the United States. The Mississippi River forms its eastern boundary. Across the river are Wisconsin and Illinois. Iowa's western border is formed by the Missouri and Big Sioux Rivers. South Dakota and Nebraska are to the west. Minnesota borders Iowa to the north, and to the south lies the state of Missouri.

Iowa is the 26th-largest state. It measures 56,273 square miles (145,746 sq km). Most of the state is flat or gently rolling plains. Its highest elevation is just 1,670 feet (509 m), at Hawkeye Point in the northwestern part of the state. Iowa's lowest point is on the Mississippi River.

An aerial view of Iowa shows the state's flat landscape, perfect for farming.

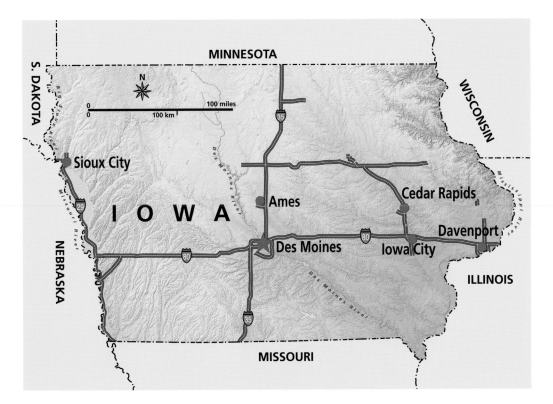

Iowa's total land and water area is 56,272 square miles (145,744 sq km). It is the 26th-largest state. The state capital is Des Moines.

Starting about 2.5 million years ago, a series of glaciers, some hundreds of feet high, covered much of Iowa. These ice sheets scoured the land. When the last glaciers melted about 10,000 years ago, they left behind flat plains and gently rolling hills.

The Ice Age glaciers also helped create some of the most fertile black soil on Earth. Most of Iowa is farmland. The state's soil is often called "The Black Gold of Iowa." When massively heavy glaciers creep across the land, they grind up the bedrock. When the ice sheets melt, they leave behind clay, sand, gravel, and pebbles. Wind and water erosion, plus centuries of composted prairie grasses, create thick layers of black soil. It is perfect for growing crops. It keeps in moisture and is rich with minerals.

Iowa has some of the most fertile black soil on Earth.

Loess Hills in western Iowa.

Not all of Iowa is flat farmland. In the northeast are rugged hills and limestone bluffs overlooking the Mississippi River. In the far western part of the state is a region called the Loess Hills. Over a period of thousands of years, windblown silt from the Missouri River Valley gathered and formed tall bluffs. The hills stretch about 200 miles (322 km) north and south along the Missouri River. This accumulated silt is called loess. (Loess is a German word that means "crumbly." It is pronounced "luss.") Today, the Loess Hills are covered with prairie grasses and woodlands. They are home to many animals, including foxes, deer, turkeys, bobcats, pheasants, and red-tailed hawks.

CLIMATE AND WEATHER

Iowa is in the middle part of the United States. It has a continental climate. Summers are hot and humid. This is good for growing crops such as corn and soybeans. In central Iowa, the growing season lasts about 162 days.

Iowa averages 34 inches (86 cm) of precipitation each year. Between 45 to 65 thunderstorms rumble over the state annually, bringing needed rain to grow crops. Spring and summer bring occasional severe weather, including high winds, hail, and tornadoes. Iowa is part of Tornado Alley. On average, twisters whirl over the state about 46 times yearly. Most are weak and do little damage, but some can be very destructive.

A massive storm strikes near Orchard, Iowa.

A homeowner clears his driveway after a December snowstorm in Urbandale.

Winters in Iowa are usually cold and snowy. The state averages about 32 inches (81 cm) of snow each year. Sometimes blizzards strike Iowa, bringing paralyzing high winds and blinding snow.

Wind often blows over Iowa's flat terrain. To prevent erosion, farmers plant rows of trees that serve as windbreaks.

PLANTS AND ANIMALS

Before European settlers arrived in the 1800s, about 70 to 80 percent of Iowa was covered with prairie grasses. Today, less than .1 percent of prairie remains. It has been replaced by farmland.

About three percent of Iowa is woodland. There are four major state forests in Iowa. They include Yellow River, Stephens, Shimek, and Loess Hills State Forests. Common trees native to Iowa include hickory, black maple, cottonwood, and black walnut. Iowa's state tree is the oak. There are about 12 species of oak that grow in the state. Bur oak trees are found throughout Iowa.

An oak tree stands in the middle of an Iowa country road.

Wildflowers grow in Iowa's woodlands and grasslands. They can also be spotted in roadside ditches and farm pastures. Iowa wildflowers include black-eyed Susans, yellow and purple coneflowers, smooth asters, tall thistles, purple prairie clover, parsley, Queen Anne's lace, and water hemlock. Iowa's official state flower is the wild rose. The flowers of the wild rose are about two inches (5 cm) wide and very fragrant. They are usually pink, but are sometimes white.

Bees and butterflies play an important part in pollinating Iowa's native plants. The butterfly garden at Bellevue State Park in eastern Iowa attracts many of the state's 60 species of butterflies. They include monarchs, buckeyes, red admirals, and tiger swallowtails.

Tiger Swallowtail

River Otter

Iowa's wild animals live in the state's woodlands or along rivers and streams. Some take refuge in farm fields. Common Iowa wildlife includes white-tailed deer, raccoons, muskrats, coyotes, squirrels, chipmunks, skunks, mink, groundhogs, rabbits, badgers, and weasels. River otters have recently been reintroduced to the state. They now thrive in many of Iowa's rivers, streams, and ponds.

Wild Turkey

Many kinds of birds are native to Iowa, or pass through during their spring and autumn migration. Birds often spotted in the state include wild turkeys, ring-necked pheasants, sparrows, quail, gray partridges, peregrine falcons, and mourning doves. The official Iowa state bird is the Eastern goldfinch. It is also called the wild canary.

Iowa is home to more than 65 kinds of amphibians and reptiles. They include blue-spotted salamanders, bullfrogs, leopard frogs, newts, skinks, mudpuppies, box turtles, wood turtles, and slender glass lizards. Common snakes include smooth green snakes, garter snakes, speckled kingsnakes, and bull snakes. Venomous snakes include copperheads and prairie rattlesnakes. Once common, prairie rattlesnakes are now rare in Iowa. They are found only in the Broken Kettle Grasslands north of Sioux City, in the northwestern part of the state.

Leopard Frog

HISTORY

The first people who lived in Iowa were the ancestors of modern Native Americans. These Paleo-Indians arrived about 13,000 years ago. They hunted animals and gathered plants.

The Woodland People first appeared about 3,000 years ago. They lived in small communities and grew crops such as corn and squash. They built huge mounds of dirt shaped like bears, deer, and birds. The earthworks were used for religious ceremonies, such as burials. Many can still be seen in Iowa today. Effigy Mounds National Monument in northeastern Iowa preserves more than 200 mounds.

An aerial view with outlines of Marching Bear Mound Group at Effigy Mounds National Monument.

A ground view of Marching Bear Mound Group.

Ma-Has-Kah, or White Cloud, an Ioway chief.

Tah-Col-O-Quoit, or Rising Cloud, a Sauk warrior.

Europeans first came to Iowa in the late 1600s. By then, several Native American tribes lived in the area. They included people from the Ioway, Santee Sioux, Oto, Missouri, and Potawatomi tribes. The powerful Sauk and Mesquaki people lived along the Mississippi River in eastern Iowa.

The first Europeans to explore Iowa arrived in 1673. They were led by Father Jacques Marquette, a French missionary, and Louis Jolliet, a French-Canadian fur trader. The expedition traveled by canoe down the Mississippi River, exploring the land as they passed by. In 1682, less than a decade later, French explorer René-Robert Cavelier, Sieur de La Salle claimed the land for France.

Modern Iowa was part of a huge territory that France called Louisiana. (Today's state of Louisiana was just a small part.) For decades, France was content to trade with Native Americans and to mine lead near today's city of Dubuque. Louisiana changed hands in 1763 when Spain took over. But France regained control in 1800.

Iowa finally became a part of the United States in 1803. President Thomas Jefferson bought Louisiana from France for a bargain price of just $15 million. It added approximately 828,000 square miles (2,144,510 sq km) of land to the country. The sale was called the Louisiana Purchase.

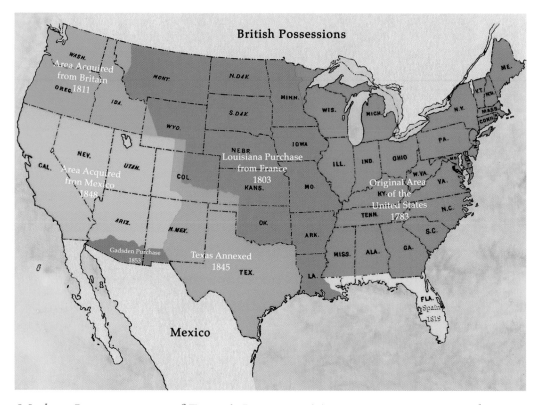

Modern Iowa was part of France's Louisiana Territory. In 1803, President Thomas Jefferson bought the huge territory from France for $15 million. The Louisiana Purchase nearly doubled the size of the new United States.

Iowa settlers found building materials scarce in the early 1800s. Many lived in sod houses. However, their lives were helped by Iowa's rich soil, which made growing crops easier.

During the early 1800s, settlers from the East crossed the Mississippi River and began farming in Iowa. The newcomers forced many Native Americans off their land. Fighting sometimes broke out. Most Native Americans were eventually forced to move onto reservations far from Iowa.

Living on the prairie was difficult for the new settlers. Wood for building houses was scarce, and prairie fires were a frequent danger. Homes were often built of sod cut from the prairie. However, these early settlers were rewarded. Crops were easy to grow in Iowa's rich soil.

The United States broke up Louisiana into smaller territories. Iowa was originally part of Missouri Territory. Then, in 1838, it became Iowa Territory. Just a few years later, in 1846, Iowa became the 29th state. Ansel Briggs was elected the first governor.

Thousands of new settlers poured into Iowa in the mid-1800s. Railroads were built across the state. Crops and other goods were shipped down the Mississippi and Missouri Rivers. River towns such as Dubuque, Davenport, Sioux City, and Council Bluffs sprang up.

The American Civil War raged from 1861 to 1865. The country was divided over slavery. Iowa sent approximately 75,000 troops to fight on the side of the Union against the pro-slavery Southern Confederacy. More than 13,000 Iowans died in the war.

In 1917, the United States entered World War I (1914-1918). Demand for food was high. Iowa farmers increased production to help the war effort.

After World War I, many Iowa farmers struggled to repay loans for farm equipment and land. The Great Depression of the 1930s made things worse. Many banks, railroads, and farms went out of business. Unemployment skyrocketed. Thousands of Iowa farmers went bankrupt and lost their land.

The economy lifted after 1941 when the United States entered World War II (1939-1945). Food from Iowa farms was in high demand again. Factories in cities like Des Moines, Ankeny, and West Burlington made ammunition and other war materials. More than 276,000 Iowans were in military service during the war.

Following World War II, Iowa remained an agricultural state. However, its cities grew. Manufacturing helped stabilize the economy. Today, Iowans are proud of their farm heritage while embracing industry and education.

A Chicago & North Western Railway train crosses a steel viaduct over the Des Moines River in Iowa.

DID YOU KNOW?

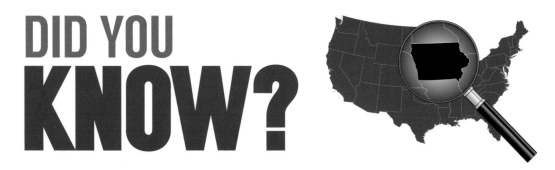

- Iowa is the only state with both western and eastern borders formed by rivers. The Mississippi River winds its way down Iowa's east side. About one-fourth of the state's western border is formed by the Big Sioux River. The remaining western border is formed by the Missouri River, which is nicknamed the "Big Muddy."

- Iowa's official state rock is the geode. These spherical rocks are found in great numbers in the southeastern part of the state, especially in the Keokuk area. They are normally about 2 to 6 inches (5 to 15 cm) in diameter. They have a hard, cauliflower-like exterior. When split open, a hollow interior is revealed, with sparkling quartz and calcite crystals.

- In the mid-1800s, many people from today's Netherlands settled in Pella and Orange City. They came to farm and find religious freedom. In 1935, the citizens of Pella organized the annual Tulip Time Festival to honor their Dutch culture. The following year, Orange City began its own Tulip Festival. Each spring, Iowans flock to the cities to marvel at thousands of beautiful flowers, parades, and folk dancing.

• The Great Flood of 1993 left parts of many Midwestern states underwater. Iowa was hit especially hard. Spring and summer rains caused the Missouri, Mississippi, Skunk, Des Moines, Cedar, Raccoon, and Iowa Rivers to overflow their banks. Many towns and farm fields were flooded. Cattle were stranded wherever they could find dry ground. Many cities, including Des Moines, were hit hard. It took several years to recover from the damage done to farms, homes, roads, and businesses. Floodwaters once again inundated Iowa in 2008, but much damage was prevented thanks to the lessons learned from 1993.

• During World War II (1939-1945), a terrible tragedy struck the Sullivan family of Waterloo, Iowa. Joseph, Francis, Albert, Madison, and George were the sons of Thomas and Alleta Sullivan. The five brothers were sailors, serving aboard the USS *Juneau* in the Pacific Ocean. They volunteered to fight, but only if they could serve together. On November 13, 1942, their ship was struck by a Japanese torpedo and sank. All five brothers were killed. The entire state of Iowa, and the nation, mourned their loss. The tragedy resulted in the military adopting the Sole Survivor Policy. It shields people from the draft or combat if a family member has already been killed in military service.

DID YOU KNOW?

PEOPLE

Herbert Hoover (1874-1964) was born in West Branch, Iowa. He became a mining engineer, and also worked to help people in Europe who suffered after World War I. In 1928, he was elected as the 31st president of the United States. He was the first president born west of the Mississippi River. As a Republican, he believed in an efficient government. He wanted to stop wasteful spending. Shortly after he took office in 1929, the Great Depression hit the country. Many businesses went bankrupt, and millions of people lost their jobs. The president tried to put people back to work on projects such as the Hoover Dam, but it wasn't enough. Hoover was defeated for reelection in 1932 by Democrat Franklin Roosevelt. Today, the Herbert Hoover Presidential Library and Museum is in West Branch.

Bob Feller (1918-2010) was a pitcher for the Cleveland Indians Major League Baseball (MLB) team for 18 seasons from the 1930s to the 1950s. He was born in Van Meter, Iowa. His pitching was so good he was nicknamed "The Heater from Van Meter." He pitched three career no-hitters, and was inducted into the Baseball Hall of Fame in 1962.

Jesse Hiatt (1826?-1898) was a pioneer who grew apples in his orchard in Madison County, Iowa. In the 1870s, a stray sapling grew between the rows of apple trees. Hiatt chopped it down twice, but it kept growing back.

Red Delicious

Finally, he let it grow. When it bore fruit, it was the sweetest apple Hiatt had ever tasted. He entered it in a contest and won. He named his apple the "Hawkeye." The name was later changed to "Red Delicious." It is one of the most popular apples sold today.

John Wayne (1907-1979) was one of Hollywood's biggest stars. Although he acted in more than 140 films, he is best remembered for his westerns. Nicknamed "The Duke," his breakthrough came in 1939 playing the Ringo Kid in director John Ford's classic western *Stagecoach*. Wayne won an

Academy Award in 1969 for his role in *True Grit*. He was also nominated for two other Academy Awards, for 1949's *Sands of Iwo Jima* and 1960's *The Alamo*. Wayne was born in Winterset, Iowa. His real name was Marion Robert Morrison, but he changed it when he went to Hollywood. Today, his childhood home is preserved in Winterset. Nearby is the John Wayne Birthplace Museum.

James Van Allen (1914-2006) was an astrophysicist who helped our early understanding of space. He was born in Mount Pleasant, Iowa. After earning advanced degrees at the University of Iowa, he became interested in space science. He conducted many experiments with satellites sent into orbit around the Earth and into space. The Van Allen radiation belts are named in his honor. He taught astronomy and physics for many years at the University of Iowa in Iowa City.

Peggy Whitson (1960-) is a NASA astronaut and biochemistry researcher. Born in Mount Ayr, Iowa, she grew up on a farm near Beaconsfield. She earned biochemistry degrees before working for NASA starting in the late 1980s. She has logged more days on the International Space Station (ISS) than any woman in NASA history. In 2007, she became the first female commander of the ISS.

CITIES

Des Moines is Iowa's capital. It is also the state's largest city. Its population is 209,220. Combined with its suburbs, it is home to about 600,000 Iowans. It is named after the Des Moines River, which runs through the heart of the city. Des Moines is known for its good schools, safe neighborhoods, and arts community. There are many outdoor sculptures and cafes downtown. Favorite attractions include the Greater Des Moines Botanical Garden, Blank Park Zoo, and the Iowa State Capitol building. The world-famous Iowa State Fair is held each August. Des Moines is a business-friendly city. It is home to many large insurance companies, banks, and financial services companies. It is also a center for health care.

Cedar Rapids is Iowa's second-largest city. Its population is 129,195. The city is a center for manufacturing, health care, and grain processing. Aviation communications company Rockwell Collins is the city's largest employer. Much of Iowa's corn passes through the city's mills, to be made into corn syrup, ethanol fuel, or feed for livestock. The biggest food employers include Quaker Oats, General Mills, and Archer Daniels Midland. Cedar Rapids also has a booming arts community. It is home to the Cedar Rapids Museum of Art, Orchestra Iowa, and the National Czech & Slovak Museum & Library. Cedar Rapids has many parks and trails on more than 4,100 acres (1,659 ha) of land.

Davenport is Iowa's third-largest city. It is located along the banks of the Mississippi River in eastern Iowa. Its population is 102,448. Together with three neighboring towns (called the Quad Cities), it is home to almost 400,000 people. Davenport's major employers include health care and manufacturing companies. The city hosts several music festivals, including the Bix Beiderbecke Memorial Jazz Festival, one of the country's largest jazz festivals. Davenport is also home to the Figge Art Museum.

Sioux City lies along the banks of the Missouri, Floyd, and Big Sioux Rivers in northwestern Iowa. Its population is 82,517. Top industries include meat processing, health care, and education. The Sioux City Lewis and Clark Interpretive Center showcases the Corps of Discovery's journey through the area.

Ames is in central Iowa. Its population is 63,266. Major industries include manufacturing, education, health care, and energy. The city is home to Iowa State University of Science and Technology. It is a major research university. Ames also hosts the National Animal Disease Center, where scientists study the health and safety of livestock and poultry.

Iowa City is in east-central Iowa. Its population is 73,415. The city hosts the University of Iowa, home of the Hawkeyes. The university is the city's biggest employer. Other major industries include health care, education, and manufacturing. Iowa City prides itself on its literary history. It is the home of the world-famous Iowa Writers' Workshop.

TRANSPORTATION

T rains began moving people and goods across Iowa in the 1840s. The first railroad bridge to cross the Mississippi River was built in 1856. It connected Illinois to the city of Davenport, Iowa. Within 10 years, railroads had stretched all the way across the state to Council Bluffs. By the early 1900s, more than 10,000 miles (16,093 km) of track crisscrossed the state. Railroads connected Iowa's farmers with markets in faraway Chicago, Illinois, and other major cities. However, it was expensive to transport goods by railroad. Today, Iowa maintains about 3,905 miles (6,284 km) of track.

Iowa has about 114,429 miles (184,156 km) of public roadways. Four major interstates cross the state. They include I-35, I-80, I-29, and I-380. Trucks use Iowa's roads to haul agricultural goods. Crops such as corn and soybeans are harvested near the state's many small towns. They are then hauled by truck to markets in larger cities.

A truck transports goods past the Barilla pasta manufacturing plant on Interstate 35 near Ames, Iowa. Many goods and crops cross Iowa's public roadways.

A barge takes goods down the Mississippi River, traveling under the Burlington Rail Bridge, near Burlington, Iowa.

Barges haul bulky cargo such as grain up and down the Missouri and Mississippi Rivers.

Iowa has 108 publicly owned airports. Each year, more than 2.5 million passengers board flights at Iowa's eight commercial airports. The busiest is Des Moines International Airport.

More than 1 million passengers fly out of Des Moines International Airport each year.

NATURAL
RESOURCES

Iowa's greatest natural resource is its rich soil. The official state soil is called Tama. It is thick, dark, and highly productive for growing crops.

About 90 percent of Iowa's land is used for agriculture. There are more than 88,000 farms in the state. Iowa is the number one grower of corn in the United States. It is used mainly to feed livestock or create ethanol fuel. Iowa also ranks number one in soybean production. Other important crops include hay, alfalfa, oats, wheat, and apples.

There are about 1,100 mining sites in Iowa. They extract limestone, sand and gravel, gypsum, and clay.

Most of Iowa's 2.1 million acres (849,840 ha) of woodlands are privately owned. The most valuable hardwood trees harvested include black walnut, white and red oak, white ash, and black cherry.

Winds often blow across the Iowa landscape. The state has put this free natural resource to work. Huge wind farms generate more than 28 percent of Iowa's electricity. That makes Iowa one of the top wind-power states in the country. Iowa wind farms generate more than 5,700 megawatts of energy, enough to power 1.5 million homes.

INDUSTRY

Iowa has diversified its economy in recent years. States that have many kinds of businesses aren't hit as hard when the national economy takes a downturn.

Manufacturing is the biggest part of Iowa's economy today. The food processing industry employs thousands of people. Iowa factories make many other products, including windows, machinery, chemicals, transportation equipment, computers and electronics, furniture, appliances, plastics, and fabricated metals.

Agriculture and related businesses make up about 33 percent of Iowa's economy. About one of every five Iowans works in the agriculture industry. The state is the nation's top producer of corn, soybeans, hogs, and eggs. It ranks in the top five in meat production.

A Waukon, Iowa, organic farmer sells an average of 2,500 eggs a week from his cage-free chickens, who roam in a fenced pasture.

Greyhound dogs race at a track near Council Bluffs, Iowa.

Iowa is strong in finance and insurance. More than 6,000 companies in these industries are located in the state. Biotechnology is also strong. Iowa scientists and researchers are always looking for ways to create new hybrid crops.

Tourism is a growing part of Iowa's economy. Many people travel from neighboring states to sample Iowa's zoos, fairs, farmers' markets, biking trails, and sporting events. Riverboat gambling, plus dog and horse racing, contributes hundreds of millions of dollars in tax revenue each year.

SPORTS

The pace of life in Iowa may be laid back, but fitness is important to the state's citizens. There are many ways to exercise outdoors, from riding bikes to simply strolling through a stand of woods with a bird-watching club. Many Iowans enjoy golf. There are more than 440 golf courses in the state. Other sports include hunting, fishing, horseback riding, soccer, canoeing, and skiing.

Bicycling has become a big sport in Iowa. RAGBRAI (Register's Annual Great Bike Ride Across Iowa) is an annual non-competitive bike ride across the state. Thousands of riders participate each year. Iowa is also busy constructing a network of bike trails throughout the state. The 25-mile (40 km) High Trestle Trail includes a section that crosses a 13-story-high bridge that spans the Des Moines River Valley.

The High Trestle Trail Bridge is a 2,530-foot (771-km) -long span near Madrid, Iowa.

Herkey the Hawk is the mascot for the University of Iowa in Iowa City.

Cy the Cardinal is the mascot for Iowa State University in Ames.

There are no major league professional sports teams in Iowa. However, high school and college sports are extremely popular. The University of Iowa, in Iowa City, is the home of the Hawkeyes. Sports teams from Iowa State University, in Ames, are called the Cyclones. The University of Northern Iowa, in Cedar Falls, and Drake University, in Des Moines, also have popular teams.

ENTERTAINMENT

The world-famous Iowa State Fair has been held each August in Des Moines since 1878. It is Iowa's largest event. It attracts more than one million visitors each year. It features rides, livestock, music, art, butter sculptures, and all kinds of food-on-a-stick.

Visitors to Urbandale's Living History Farms learn 300 years of Iowa history in a 500-acre (202 ha) outdoor museum. There are three working farm sites and a pioneer town, complete with a blacksmith and general store.

The Amana Colonies include seven villages that were first settled in the mid-1800s by German immigrants. Located near Iowa City, the site preserves many original buildings.

The National Farm Toy Museum in Dyersville displays thousands of scale models and toys. The museum has one of the largest cast-iron farm toy collections in the world.

Blank Park Zoo in Des Moines displays hundreds of animals on 49 acres (20 ha) of land. The Grotto of the Redemption is found in West Bend. Each year, thousands of people visit this shrine made of rock, gems, and glass. The DeSoto National Wildlife Refuge in western Iowa preserves habitat for many birds and animals.

Misha, an Amur tiger native to Russia, plays in the snow at the Blank Park Zoo.

The Iowa State Fair, held every August, is considered one of the best in the nation.

TIMELINE

1673—Father Jacques Marquette and Louis Jolliet paddle down the Mississippi River and visit Iowa.

1682—All land bordering the Mississippi River (including Iowa) is claimed for France by explorer René-Robert Cavelier, Sieur de La Salle.

1788—Lead is mined by Julien Dubuque in Iowa.

1803—The United States buys the Louisiana Territory from France. The deal is called the Louisiana Purchase. The land includes modern-day Iowa.

1838—Iowa Territory is established. It includes parts of what are now Iowa, North Dakota, South Dakota, and Minnesota.

1846—Iowa becomes the 29th state.

1929-1939—Many farms are lost during the Great Depression.

1957—*The Music Man* debuts on Broadway. The play is written by Iowa native Meredith Willson, from Mason City.

1973—The first RAGBRAI bike tour takes place, with participants riding from Sioux City to Davenport.

1988—The baseball fantasy movie *Field of Dreams* is filmed near Dyersville, Iowa.

1993—Massive flooding causes billions of dollars of damage. The disaster becomes known as the Great Flood of 1993.

2007—Iowa native and professional golfer Zach Johnson wins his first major golf tournament, the Masters.

2008—Barack Obama wins the Iowa Democratic Caucuses, the first step on his way to becoming president.

2015—The Iowa Hawkeyes football team, from the University of Iowa, has one of its best seasons in recent history. Its 12-1 record (8-0 in the Big Ten) earns the team a trip to the Rose Bowl in Pasadena, California.

GLOSSARY

GLACIER

A huge, slow-moving sheet of ice that grows and shrinks as the climate changes. The ice sheets can be more than one mile (1.6 km) thick.

GREAT DEPRESSION

A time in American history beginning in 1929 and lasting for several years when many businesses failed and millions of people lost their jobs.

HYBRID

A combination of two kinds of plants or animals. Hybrid crops are very common. Agriculture researchers try to combine different types of plants to create new crops that taste better, grow bigger, or are drought and insect resistant.

LEWIS AND CLARK EXPEDITION

An exploration of western North America, led by Meriwether Lewis and William Clark, from 1804-1806.

LIMESTONE

A hard rock used to construct buildings and in making lime and cement. Limestone is formed from the remains of shells or coral.

LOUISIANA PURCHASE

The purchase by the United States of about 828,000 square miles (2,144,510 sq km) of land from France in 1803.

PLAIN

A large, flat area of land.

POLLINATION

The act of transferring pollen from one part of a plant to another part of the same or another plant so that the plant can produce seeds.

PRAIRIE

An ecosystem that includes grasses and flowering plants. Most of the plant roots are deep under the surface. It takes many years for prairies to form. Frequent fires burn off dead material and return nutrients to the soil. Deep-rooted plants then re-sprout. This cycle of death and regrowth forms rich, black soil over many thousands of years.

ROTATE

To move crops to different areas of land in order to keep the soil fertile and productive.

SOD

The top surface of prairie soil, with grass growing on the surface and roots embedded underneath.

TORNADO ALLEY

An area of the United States that has many tornadoes. Tornado Alley stretches from Texas in the south to North Dakota in the north and east to parts of Ohio.

VAN ALLEN RADIATION BELTS

Layers of radioactive particles that circle planets that have magnetic poles. The Earth has two main radiation belts. They are dangerous to the electronic equipment on satellites if the spacecraft spend too much time flying within them. They are named after Iowan James Van Allen, the astrophysicist who confirmed their existence in 1958.

INDEX